Scattered Allegories

Ohan Hominis

Published by Unsolicited Press
www.unsolicitedpress.com
Copyright © 2016 Ohan Hominis
All Rights Reserved.
Unsolicited Press Books are distributed to the
trade by Ingram.
ISBN: 978-0-9980872-6-9

Poems

Anybody Can Do It

"I want to write her a poem
to tell her how much I love her"

he said

"but I'm no poet
I don't have a way with words
I stumble
along
fidgeting with my grammar
and it always ends up silly.
I can't make it look easy
can't make it sound natural
but I try.
I haven't sent her a text message
that didn't take me hours
because I scrutinize every word.

'Hi'
Takes me an hour and a half.
How it reads in my head,
how it sounds when I read it out loud,
what it looks like backlit
on a little phone screen.
I sometimes read my own messages
to her
on her phone
while she's sleeping
to see if the words look like I thought they
would,
that's how much I love her.

I knew everything had to be perfect.
That I had to be the absolute best version
of myself
if I ever wished to keep her
interested.

I don't want to write about her hair, oh,
it's perfect but I don't want to write about it.
Or her smile,
her ears when she laughs,
and when she's not laughing,
or her nose
anything about her,
she's perfect.
How could I focus on any of her?
I'd be better off handing her an anatomy
textbook
and saying
here,
these are all the things about you that are
perfect.
Hand her a map
with all the beautiful places cut out of it
and say
I'd go anywhere for you.

But I don't want something cheesy like sunsets,
she's so much better than a poem about
sunsets,
she's so much better than sunsets.
I want to write her the poem she deserves,
because then I'd have something to show for it.
For the time.
Because hours spent in flower shops

looking for the least not quite perfect bouquet
don't quite sum it up,
even though I'm allergic to pollen,
and always come back itchy.
It doesn't quite explain
how much I love her,
how I would change everything about the world
if it meant she wouldn't even change
one atom of her being."

And all the while I,
with a smile on my face,
waited for him to finish spontaneously reciting
the first draft of his poem.

A Poet's View

Give a poet a window to look out of
and a set of eyes to look into
and they will create.

The walled in poet with no view of nature,
to see their reflection,
has no context beneath their ideas.

The lonely poet with no view of a heart,
to understand their own,
has no passion behind their words.

Give a poet a window to look out of
and they will tell you what they see.
Give a poet a set of eyes to look into
and there is nothing they won't set free.

What will I see when I look out your window,
What will I see when I look into your eyes.
What poetry goes on outside your home
What poetry goes on inside your mind.

Let me see through your perspective
Let me live in your soul.
And I might lift you towards your dreams
And I might help you towards your goals.

I would lay down on your sill
I would make your cheekbones my pews.
So your mind could drive my will.
So your eyes could be my view.

This Morning

Morning,
faint fog floats faithfully along
as the forest breathes,
air still thick from owning the night.
The birds began calling
and only the first of men have woken.

Good morning,
steaming tea sits steeping situated in front of me
and for a few moments I feel the world wait,
weighted with lighthearted anticipation,
for me to take the first sip
so the day might unfold.

This morning
I pause for a few extra moments
earth nesting tension, testing nature,
knowing the tea will be that much stronger
that the cricket will chirp that much louder
that the squirrel will have more ground to gain
once he begins.

For mornings
are the best time to appreciate all that is done
while humanity rests,
and I wake up every day with renewed vigor
eagerly awaiting the role set aside for me
knowing instinct will be my director.

But this morning
I take a few extra moments to think of you

hoping that if the entire world waits with me,
for the exhale of my deep breath,
it might have enough time to reach you
untainted
and fall into place beneath your wings.

My Head in Your Lap

i lay there
here
my head in your lap
forever in
your lap
as music from the speakers fills the room
your breath captures my attention
amidst the whispering of the fountains outside
the humming of the spring breeze
chasing the waning sunlight through the window
the flickering candle on the sill
the incense
your hair spilling wildly over my pages
my hand writing these words through it anyway
the music softens
your face comes into view
and beauty
the likes of which could never be contained by
words
consumes the present moment

Heartbeat

There is something about listening
to the heartbeat of someone you love,
pressing your head into their chest
and feeling them breathe,
feeling life flow from the heaven you share
into their lungs, heart, veins, lips,
you kiss mine
and suddenly I've lost my breath,
turns out the air is much thinner in the clouds,
before I inhale luscious soulfulls of you
and am grounded again by the wonders
of the earth around us,

how beautiful Eden is,
my favorite place to go apple picking,
as in the distance birds chirp,
winds rustle leaves through trees,
and the thumping of your heart
draws my ear to the fertile earth of your body
to listen to the sounds of my own heart's sweet
surrender,

and though the god of time occasionally gathers
its will
to throw us out of our ageless realm,
it only helps create our notion of bliss,
for our time apart is the pedestal on which
heaven is built,
what good is eternity
if it is but the infidelity of need and urgency
when the emergence of them

births our greatest expressions of passion,
the ephemeral works of art that love is forged
from,

so let the instances of our distance be
for as exchanged heartbeats define our unity,
it is those spent apart that weave its tapestry.

Painter of Past Dreams

The tree
we had paused at,
its interwoven branches not unlike our bodies
earlier that day
or, was it with another woman i have loved?
i've known each wholly,
it's only that they are all etched into my memory
by the greatest painter of past dreams
my mind has to offer,
and that her work,
made with the finest tools
and given shape in the most expert
craftsmanship,
comprises the exquisite gallery
that lay upon a golden hilltop in my mind
where only the sun ever shines
and birds forever sing
and flowers bloom eternally,
and that i'm left
in perpetual awe
as i walk through the gilded halls
not of the works of art themselves,
but of the immense passion from which they
were forged
and the incomparable series of muses
under which my universe itself
takes shape.

Ode to the Moon

Man will compose symphonies
paint frescos
write volumes of poetry
attempting to capture

the beauty of a sunset
the frailty of a flower
the fortitude of a mountain
or the ferocity of a storm

the organization of the ant
the grace of the eagle
the dominion of the lion
or the sovereignty of the whale,

Man
will perpetually strive
to perfect his imitation of nature
to validate his existence

as he destroys
what he cannot claim
and lays waste to that
which evades his capture,

while Woman
with the combined poise
of all that has ever been worthy
of immortalization through art

and with the grace

of the earth itself
will humbly
give birth to him.

To Sky, From Beast

I want to lose my mind in your body,
let instincts take hold in the ensuing craze
and attain the enlightenment
of the first man to tame fire,

I would play your humble terrestrial wanderer,
to hunt and gather bits of your soul
until I have enough to break ground
and take root,
learn to satisfy my curious hungry demons
on the fertile fields of your body,

I long to chart the constellations of your being,
look to your eyes to discover my truths
with every shift in your attention
being a change in my seasons,
waiting for you to fall from balanced heavens
so I might reap our bounty
and sacrifice it to you at your altar,

I dream to dance in the mounting smoke
that rises to the skies
and carve cave paintings of the moment it
touches your horizons
with eager fingers into the grooves of your skin,
then thrust forth spear in hand to hunt
and devour the flesh that is of you,

For what am I but beast looking up at his night
sky,
praying for cleansing rain

to wash off this subtle sentience
and emerge from your planet hearth,
a budding artist from the ashes of feral brute,
so that I might look back in wonder
at my own unlikely evolution,
and sit down, pen in hand,
to write of it.

Blond Curls

blond curls
these thick
blond
curls
that's all i remember
you see i was honestly sober
but these wild thighs
took hold of my attention
and i
melted away
rigidly
i mean i froze
but started to sway
dazed at the sight of those
metronome hips
one look and i take sips on her existence
gold wisps are all i subsist on
as gibberish dances across my lips

what did i say to this goddess
that lured her from her palace
and let me drink from her chalice
i don't feel eternal
but something about it lasted for lifetimes
what absolved me from the crimes i've
committed
to be allowed past the gates into heaven

i'm still finding feathers in my sheets
how considerate leaving me souvenirs to keep
of the one time i'll ever get a taste of outer space

had her legs on my shoulders and I felt
weightless
diving into seas of sweet bliss
soaring in skies of crescendoing cries
of untethered happiness

cue the trumpets
i made love with some angel from above
carved kama sutra in cuneiform
into the mattress
and the floor
and the dresser
and the couch in the living room
the shower
the bathroom sink
the kitchen sink
the counter

if apartments could talk
mine would tell a story like cave paintings
detailing a creation myth

with all the passion and glory
of two sides clashing in storied
tales of wails of delight
reaching heavenly heights

i think i'll start it with

once upon a time
these blond curls
these
damn
blond
curls

Moon in the Water

When I think of her it's always water,
the warm waveless sea of a sheltered bay
that only footpaths lead to,
with a tree line that shyly dips to taste
the welcoming surf
as it playfully tumbles onto the sand,
before rolling back, sensually,
reminding you that she is part of the ocean,

and even in the daylight reflecting the moon,
the serene beauty of dusk and dawn,
like a kiss on the nape of your neck
while your lips lie in waiting,
I can still imagine floating in her
as she'd lift my body away
with her engulfing embrace
into the warm bliss of weightlessness,

before I would turn to drink deep,
attempting to swallow her every drop,
as my lips danced in her bounty
while still drowning in the luxury of abundance,
for how can one man match, even engorged,
the satiation of the depths of the pool of life.
Somewhere in time I still lay on her shores,
fulfilled, as her waves lick at my body.

Inspiration

I glance at you from over the brim of my book
pen in hand as you undress at the foot of my
bed
you catch me staring,
admiring your casual elegance
with anyone else looking through my blindless
windows.

I watch a smile swim across your lips
at the sight of the madman narrating his
appreciation of you,
sprawled out nude below the neck
face covered by pages filled with his own words
save for his eyes
and frayed hair curled in every direction.

What is love if not the ability to be amused by
eccentricity,
how long can you watch me watching you watch
me as I watch you
and what does all that watching amount to,
how telling of time past in one another's
company.

I think you sense how annoyed you'd be at the
last verse
because you've started crawling
on all fours
towards me
the mischievous smile that makes me rush these
words knowingly,

I scrawl thoughts hurriedly as you linger
longingly
pawing casually
at sensitive places on my body to distract me.

I know,
the pen knows,
what limited time it has left
before the mind that drives it
is drained of blood as passion
defines the present moment
and we dive into it
bodies entwined

– but wait

I'm not done yet,
not ready to start
though
your lips hover over my neck
as your hands reach for my book
and I wri-

To Winged Cherubs

A stone statue of a winged cherub
wrestling an eagle
sits gracefully,
peacefully locked in eternal struggle
in a bed of blooming begonias.

A grayed couple,
veterans of many springtime,
sit behind it,
and slightly to the left,
in the shade of a white birch tree.

The sun lines the pathway
flanked by fragrant bushes
and colorful flowerbeds
as light breezes brush playfully between their
ranks.

I walk,
arm in arm with my own sweetheart
just another fifty pleasant years till she and I,
whomever she may be,
sit, quietly,
everything to say already having been said,
behind, and slightly to the left,
of some other cherub
with his own endless tale of potential glory.

But now,
still young like the buds of springtime
with so much yet to express,

whisper and nuzzle lovingly
like the roots to the earth beneath our feet,
while clouds pass by
in their never-ending march
towards bliss.

The Future Proceeds

The scenery flies by
like time itself
I'm unable to enjoy it all
as your hair flows behind us
a trail of the receding memories
of cities past.

The midday sun shines above
beginning its long descent
into the horizon
as we chase it
on the coattails of a spinning earth.

You look at me
behind reflective lenses
that show me my own reaction
to your smile
bright and alive
and lingering behind
is a longing not yet discovered.

I stare back at you
the world unraveling in my peripheral vision
as we fly past state lines
running free
to what we don't yet know
and from what we will never admit.

And in that moment I love you.
I love you like the country drifting past us
the temporary perfection of this moment

captured by your posture
more beautiful than any view
your own mountains and valleys
rivaling the best of what nature can offer.

I marvel at your existence
as you reach for my hand
and in that moment I am content
and for once
I love myself.

Gifts

some gifts are too precious to keep,
their weight sits like lead
in the bottom of our hearts,
presses down on our lungs
and engulfs our thoughts,
with calls to nostalgia like the siren song
towards the jagged rock of time's irreconcilable
nature,
hollow reminders of the love that bore them,
shadows of bliss,
light clouds weighed down by rain
blotting out a once blue sky,
mountains covered by ocean depths of soul,
those whose thought bares thorns unseen
born of the struggle with impermanence,
memories too heavy to carry
and so too often cut loose,
unless we escape from under the sorrow,
grasp all that is precious in the gift
and in discarding the longing
carve out the beautiful
and cherish it.

A Rose To Admire

I will find you,
pull you out from the rubble of soul
and the mountain of sand
time continues to pour between us,

come back to me,
back to finding meaning in the world,
so we can again share our sunrises and sunsets,
our blooming flowers and cleansing rain,
back to knowing that all is bliss
and that no thing can't outweigh nothingness,

we are both dying,
for life begets death,
and though it is the well from which life draws
its beauty
I can no longer watch you drown in thirst,

welcome again with me the subtlety of every
moment
and give up living subtley, in no moments at all,
projecting only shadows of yourself as you fade
in the flush,

I will run,
barefoot and wild,
the earth beneath my soles
and open sky above,
with arms outstretched
and the wind bracing my skin
to remind you of the wonders of breathlessness,

watch me trudge
bleeding and broken
through the desolate desert of desperation,
longing only for the present moment
with you,
tending to the wounded sleeves that once held
my heart
in search of that oasis of experience,
subsisting on simply existing,
only so you might again see your own worth,

I will remind you what it is to know the smell of
flowers
as well as the smell of fresh earth
so that every time you are trodden down,
clutching at the ground in your attempts to
stand,
you can find yourself a rose to admire
and wait again in your unyielding beauty
for me to find you.

The Sound of Rain

She was in my bones.
I wrote a volume
to the melody of her memory
playing in my mind
hoping I could coax her
into the spine of the tome
and be rid of the weight
her beauty rested on my shoulders.

She had commandeered
the rights to every sound
I witnessed in her presence.
Not the chirping of birds,
nor the sound of rain, or rushing wind,
were mine any longer.
They belonged, as I did,
to her, their lost conductor,
before being left with the shadow
of our once symphony.

I wandered, discordant,
looking for harmony in any body
but I was numb to every pitch.
I shook, vibrating to the dissonance,
hearing only my echoes
for I was so utterly alone
in the muted vastness of her absence.

Tending Fires

Just saw an old friend
she has a kid now
a son
and she's pregnant again
twins it seems
it was only yesterday
that I was biting on her nipples
in the bathroom of a dive bar
on the lower east side
with her hand down my pants
oh where the time goes
we got kicked out that night
when they found us
having a laugh with the bouncer
on our way to the door
he wished he didn't have to
put us out on the street
to the flashing lights
and the honking horns
in the late hours
of a Saturday night
among fellow revelers
who cheered us on
as it started to rain
and she pinned me
against the graffiti on a wall
that also no longer exists
but that street corner does exist
and I do
and she does
in a way at least

like all things do
in the illusion of the present moment
as the past recedes
into alleyways of the mind
where the graffiti fades
at a slower pace
and recollections of old
lovers and friends
tend their ever shrinking fires
in the cold unforgiving night
of memory.

That Night with the Fog

do you remember that night with the fog.
that night when the sea and sky were the same
color
and shades of grays then blues then blacks
dominated the horizon?
when the boats were floating somewhere on the
edge of the world,
with the wind chiming of anchored ships
among the midnight flapping of geese.

remember being watched by the shimmering
trails of lights in the distance
from cities we would never know,
when you kissed me in the mist at night
with only the gas lamps,
dotting the pier like stars,
to keep us company?

do you remember that night when we were
passing comets?
how the brief pinks of sunset danced upon the
woolen sky for a moment
before soaking up the darkness of a sunless sea,
and we crossed in our meandering orbits
towards fates we could not know,
to eclipse one another to the moon, the pier, the
skies, the sea,
and for an instant collide?

do you remember that night,
was it yesterday or tomorrow,

in this life or next,
have the years gone by and been kind to you
or am I a part of your pending memories?

there was fog that night,
amidst the little town on the water
and the life that surrounds it.
I can still feel your breath on my neck,
still taste the love on your lips.
I wonder,
do you remember that night?
and am I with you?

Library

Floor to ceiling shelving leather bound books
sherry cigars cognac fireplaces smell of wood
heat warmth of the fire shag of a rug stuffing of
the couch you the smell of your hair the plump
of your lips taste of your skin the sound of
music scent of books the paint on the ceiling gilt
of the chandelier the reflection of marble the feel
of your hands nape of your neck the treble of
your voice bass of my heart the button of your
nose warmth your stomach full of butterflies
senses flooded threaded into memory by the
emotion of being with you the endless string of
thoughts turned poetry captured by the books
around us embodied by our bound bodies
encapsulating the embroidered tapestry of our
library lounge garden full of art of the nature of
your mind.

Midnight Wife

I see you,
taunting me with your curves
flaunting to me your smile
my ephemeral beauty.
Come closer.

I don't need your permanent love,
nor a shared life,
I just need you for this one night
to be my midnight wife.

I want to build sandcastles
with you
in a room,
love as beautiful as it ever has been
washed away by the morning tide of time's
passing.

I want to paint with you
our memories
on the walls of an empty building
ready for demolition,
until the inevitability of its destruction comes to
fruition.

Let the present be our canvas
on which we paint our mural,
let the temporary be our repository
for the etchings something purer,

I want not for time to tarnish

what I feel for you now.
Let your voice flourish in my mind
as the trophy of my prime,

I want you to be the what-if of my dreams
the muse to my eternal schemes.
You deserve to run, free,
uninhibited by decree,

I need a wind.
Fuel me,
Fan my spirit,
let me engulf you with my soul
as you challenge me continually

let me love you,
forever always as now,
drifting behind my eyes
as I smile into another's
be my secret.

I feel you.
Taunting me with your curves
flaunting to me your smile
my ephemeral beauty,
come closer.

Serendipity

How many poems have I scrawled onto your
body?
This may be the first I've written down
but I've spoken countless into your skin,
whispering wordlessness to your senses,
essences phrases could never capture.
Making love to you is my favorite art form.

Countless reliefs sculpted into your limbs,
frescoes painted with my lips,
symphonies composed through your vocal
chords,
but the truth is all this striving for physical bliss
is not even the half of it,
for it's your mind that drives me,
your relentless curves may keep me breathless
but it's your encephalon I'm hooked on.

Day dreaming of cerebral romances,
our neural dances where we debate
the best ways to promulgate our thoughts,
with a passion wrought from friendship
before attraction engendered some
additional possibilities,
like the chance for me
to massage the parts of your mind
my words can't reach
but to which through your body
I might manage to speak.

You've made me feel like an artist

who himself plays muse
to a profuse starlet
feeding off the inspiration
flowing from the daily culmination
of our intertwined collaboration
in striving for mutual satiation.

What a fortunate date with serendipity
that our eyes met,
for through them into your mind I saw
the beauty that enchanted me.
And you must forgive that this will forever
remain a draft,
I promise to write you more as time continues to
pass,
but for a first attempt it will have to suffice
as I could labor for eternity without getting it
right.

Taken From the Sea

How do you describe the moonlight that shines
through branches
and gives halos to leaves
before falling onto warm tropical sand?

The bits of ocean that linger in hair
and beneath fingernails.
The sweat dwelling on the nape of your neck,
your silken sun kissed legs.

The ebony of your body calling to me like the sea
at night,
the rise and fall of your chest like the tide.

How do you describe ephemeral beauty?
And can we just call it bliss.

Early morning mosques serenade the moon
as crickets compete with the early birds
over the rolling of thunder in the distance.

I come back in a daze to your night sky skin
glistening like surf
so I might pray to my taste of the divine.

Light rain starts its drumming on the thatched
roof
as I wrap my body around yours
and consume you,
beneath the mosquito net,
with only the fan as our persistent witness.

For You, the Sunsets and Sea Breezes

that sunsets, sea breezes, and temples in prayer
should remind me of you,
that it is forever in the baths
in the remoteness
of our shared experience
that we should cohabit a space,
so curated by us
that it requires perfection within which to
unfold,
is, in itself, a reason to create,
to furnish other rooms of us
decorated in swaths color and life,
our palates having dined on
east village murals
mosques on the Bosphorous
and full moons on the emerald isle,
to say nothing of the countless sunsets
with waves washing up to coast
a long string of memories welded
to the shores of our joint reality.

where else but the moon to shoot for,
carving out seline craters
to house our lunar seas of dreams
while we're left embracing in the serene,
our conversations astral
plain speech between us
reaching beyond the firmament
to unravel one another

and weave a unified testament
of unspoken words,
that rhythmic language tapped out by beating
hearts.

as we trip across realms held aloft
by the peaks of our design,
my mind sails on the grooves of our sonorous
dance
to record the harmony in your every move,
you are the music played by music,
the choreophile wave to my logonaut pilot,
graphing our entwined plot
as I navigate the unyielding rhapsody,
the personified verse,
that is
your entire being.

I love you to the ends of my cognition,
to the limits of my ability to express,
where every attempt to verbalize
pushes my mind to its brink,
to the wordless stammering of the overwhelmed,
the blathering nothingness of unnamable
sentiment,
knowing each word flown from tear ducts
is worth a thousand drops pulled from the mind,
to look through my rapture
and see emotion welling over
in the obsidian pools
of my heart's sweet desire,
and be flooded with acknowledgement,
the disarming relief of relinquished self-reliance
in the face of reciprocated passion,
that surrogate home of unimpeachable trust,

and be enveloped by the solace of your embrace,
and breathe in you.

Curtains

I still flash back to that anticipation
as I made my way to the shower
where she was waiting for me,
knowing I'd find her body
nude and glistening
under the rushing water,
before I pulled back the curtain
and stepped in as she turned
almost shyly
to place her hands on my thighs
and inch closer.
The feel of her supple flesh
releasing mine from
what could have been eons
of pressure built up
from our time apart.
I almost shiver
when I think about pressing her against the tiles
our voices echoing off them in ecstasy
before the cyclone of our bodies hit the bed
soaked and panting
and we bore a hole into it
digging into one another
while my suit pounced on her empty dress
somewhere on the floor beneath us
and our shoes continued to dance the night
away.

The Creaking Bed

the creaking bed.
I keep telling her I'll fix it,
it's definitely the screws.
the thud thud thud against the wall
sends the painting floating above my head
rattling
only slightly slower than the
pattering
of my heart.

I focus on the curve of her neck
down into the wells of her collarbones
where her thick curled hair
pools in a body
I could swim in for an eternity.

she leaves me for a moment,
panting,
my body nailed to the bed
as my consciousness
floats around the room with her.

I drift,
carelessly,
admiring simple things
like the starkness of bare white walls
as rapture runs through my veins.

the old raw wood of her studio
doesn't even creak
as she crosses the large open space,

floating past tall windows
a floor
and a half
above the city streets
in a story all her own.

her nude silhouette
blows over to the bed
like a draft from the panes
and she's back,
the silk of her skin
like a breeze
brushing against my body.

my skin crawls all over
attempting to leave my human form
to join her heavenly one
just to be part of something
greater.

I press my lips to her cheek
as I float down the luscious stream of her curves
to drink
from the fountain of youth.

waves crash above me
as I lap at the creek flowing
from the hearth of human existence
and I
am alive.

standing tall
I breach the cave of being
and crash through the allegory
scattering shadows around the room

that debate with us
the universal truths
as we are thrown
into the ephemeral cosmic bliss,
and we,
existing from moments such as this,
lay back
and drift
on the simple knowledge
of each other's presence.

I curl my hands over hers
to make sure I don't get
swept away.

Home

what is home
I can't help but wonder
as the end of our time
together
draws near,

and memories of you flood
weighted meditations
of daily exhaustion,
the steady mounting
of life's extant weariness.

warm thoughts curled up beside me
in my cold bed
are of you,
inherent nostalgic longings for home
all end up renovated
all end up looking
a lot like your body.

what is home
I ask myself
brushing away mother's nest
for sake of progress,
I realize my home is silliness,
is late night wanderings
in closed off parks,
early morning romps
through still sleeping neighborhoods,
home is playful collusion
in committing crimes

drawn up with childlike innocence.

what is home
if not
massages when you don't need them,
midnight picnics
on bedroom floors
by candlelight,
drawn out showers
that make us both late,
reading poems to one another
in midday about sunset,
at night about sunrise.

I love you like nostalgia
tying itself to the masts
of memory's sinking ship,
like dew,
clung to grass
drawing its last breath
as dawn draws near.

what is home
you must be it because
I can't help but run
from your comfort,
can't help but long
for your particular warmth
enveloping my shivering bones,
can't replicate the beauty
of the simple bliss
of existing next to you.

what is home
I wonder

as I take my first step
towards time's tragedy
of our parting hearts.

what is home
as I wander,
what is home?

Made in the USA
Charleston, SC
28 December 2016